AF688159

AI Personal Assistants 101

Create Your Own 24/7 Assistant Using ChatGPT, Notion & Make

By Joe Correa

Published by Live Stronger Faster

Copyright © 2025 by Joe Correa

All rights reserved.

No part of this publication may be reproduced, distributed, or transmitted in any form or by any means—electronic, mechanical, photocopying, recording, or otherwise—without the prior written permission of the publisher, except in the case of brief quotations embodied in critical reviews and certain other noncommercial uses permitted by copyright law.

This book is for educational and informational purposes only. The author and publisher are not engaged in rendering legal, financial, or other professional advice. Readers should consult a qualified professional before making any financial decisions.

First Edition

Table of Contents

Introduction

The idea of having your own personal assistant used to belong only to CEOs, celebrities, and people with massive corporate support. It required hiring staff, training them, paying salaries, and managing personalities. Today, everything has changed. A single individual working from home—using nothing more than ChatGPT, a laptop, and a few no-code tools—can build a personal AI assistant that works day and night, never forgets anything, never complains, never loses energy, and never needs time off. This book exists because the world has entered a new era where technology doesn't just simplify life—it extends your mind, multiplies your productivity, and expands your potential far beyond human limits. Your first AI personal assistant will not just take tasks off your plate; it will permanently transform your capacity to work, create, think, organize, and operate in the world.

Most people think of AI assistants as simple chatbots or playful tools that can answer questions and generate quick replies. But a true personal AI assistant does far more than respond to prompts. It thinks ahead. It reminds you of things before you forget them. It organizes your schedule, plans projects, structures goals, analyzes content, summarizes research, drafts messages, manages tasks, and even connects with your favorite apps through automation. This book will show you how to build an assistant that doesn't just react—it anticipates your needs. It becomes your second brain, your executive partner, and the invisible force that keeps your entire life aligned, optimized, and under control.

AI personal assistants are no longer futuristic science fiction—they are the new baseline for operating in a high-speed world. The volume of information modern life demands from us is overwhelming. We manage emails, messages, scheduling, research, projects, documents, PDFs, content creation, finances, reminders, tasks, obligations, and responsibilities spread across dozens of apps. The human brain wasn't designed to manage this much input. That's why overwhelm has become normal. But overwhelm is no longer a requirement. When you build a personalized AI assistant that centralizes everything, organizes it, processes it, and acts on it automatically, your entire life becomes simpler, faster, and more powerful. You begin to feel like you're operating with a support system you always wished you had but could never afford—until now.

This book focuses on building an AI personal assistant using ChatGPT, Notion, and Make, because these three tools form the perfect no-code triangle. ChatGPT acts as the thinking engine—your AI's brain. Notion becomes the memory system—a dynamic database where notes, tasks, calendars, and projects live and interact. Make connects everything together—the automation engine that triggers actions, moves information, updates databases, and keeps everything flowing. When you learn how to combine all three, you unlock a level of assistive power that feels almost magical. You give your AI the ability to read your data, monitor your responsibilities, send messages, update your calendar, manage your tasks, and keep your entire workflow synchronized.

In this series, Book 1 helped you build your first AI agent. But Book 2 goes deeper. It focuses on the human side of AI—your life, your habits, your mental load, your goals, your routines, and the systems that define your personal world. Your AI assistant will become a partner in everything you do. It will help you wake up with clarity, work more efficiently, manage your day without chaos, and go to sleep knowing that nothing slipped through the cracks. Once you build your first scheduling assistant, task manager, research bot, or automated message responder, you begin to understand why AI personal assistants are not a luxury. They are a life upgrade. They help you think better, decide better, live better, and stay organized without effort.

Throughout this book, you will build multiple assistants—each with a specific purpose. You'll create an AI that plans your schedule based on priorities, automates time blocking, and organizes your week with precision. You'll build a task-management assistant that captures new tasks, categorizes them, and sends them into Notion automatically. You'll build a research assistant that can collect information from the web, summarize PDFs, search databases, create reports, and send you insights on autopilot. You'll build messaging bots that respond to leads, clients, customers, or community members using pre-approved templates and brand-aligned communication. Each assistant will be simple to build, but shockingly powerful once operational.

By the end of this book, you won't just understand how AI personal assistants work—you will have multiple assistants running in your life, handling responsibilities you used to stress about. You will know how to assign tasks to your AI like you would assign them to a human. You will know how to automate workflows that used to take you hours. You will know how to create a "life operating system" powered by AI that keeps you organized without requiring your constant attention. You will discover how to build assistants that think with you, for you, and ahead of you. And ultimately, you will experience the feeling of having space—mental space, emotional space, time space—to focus on what matters most.

This book is part of a larger vision: empowering people to build their own AI agents, assistants, tools, and automations without writing a single line of code. Technology should not require a technical background. It should not be reserved for programmers. It should belong to everyone. Whether you are a business owner, student, creator, freelancer, employee, or entrepreneur, AI assistants can elevate your life instantly. And once you build them yourself—once you see the inner logic, customization, and automation—you will realize you are not just using AI tools. You are building intelligent systems. You are engineering workflows. You are designing assistants that work exactly the way you want. You are taking control of your time and future at a level few ever achieve.

The journey you begin with Book 2 is more personal than the others. It is not just about creating bots or automations. It is about creating a better version of your daily life. A more structured version. A more peaceful version. A more productive version. A version of you that has bandwidth for growth instead of drowning in to-dos. This is where your AI becomes more than a tool—it becomes a teammate. And once that happens, you will never want to live without it again.

Chapter 1

The Architecture of a Personal AI Assistant

Building a personal AI assistant is not about connecting random tools together or simply prompting ChatGPT to behave like a helper. A true personal AI assistant is an engineered system—a structured combination of memory, reasoning, logic, instructions, automations, workflows, triggers, and data storage. In this chapter, you will learn the essential architecture that every powerful AI personal assistant must have before you start building specialized assistants later in the book. Without this foundation, your systems will become messy, unpredictable, and difficult to scale. With the right foundation, your AI assistant becomes reliable, organized, consistent, and capable of running at a level that feels almost like magic. The purpose of this chapter is to give you that foundation.

Your personal AI assistant begins with three core components: the brain, the memory, and the automation engine. These are represented by ChatGPT, Notion, and Make. ChatGPT acts as the reasoning engine—it interprets your instructions, generates responses, understands context, and makes decisions based on what you want the assistant to achieve.

Notion is the structured memory system where your tasks, projects, notes, lists, schedules, ideas, and reference materials live. Make becomes the connective tissue that moves information between apps, triggers actions, updates databases, runs workflows, and orchestrates everything behind the scenes. When these three components come together, your AI assistant becomes capable of operating as a system rather than a standalone tool.

Every personal AI assistant must start with a clear role definition. This is the assignment of identity and responsibility. Most people skip this step, but it is the single most important element of building an AI that behaves predictably. When you give your assistant a role, you give it purpose. You define how it should think, what it should prioritize, how it should respond, and how it should interpret requests. A "scheduling assistant," "task manager," "research bot," "communications assistant," or "document analyst" each think and behave differently because their role definitions shape their decision-making. In this book, you will learn to write effective role prompts that include objectives, personality, constraints, data sources, logic rules, and decision frameworks. This transforms your AI from a general-purpose chatbot into a specialized system with a clear identity.

Once the role is defined, the next component is the operating system—your structured framework for how the assistant navigates information. This involves creating organized databases in Notion, such as a task database, calendar database, project dashboard, habit tracker, journal, or resource library. The structure of these databases determines how your assistant stores information, retrieves it, analyzes it, and organizes it. A poorly structured database leads to confusion and disorganization. A well-designed database becomes the backbone of your personal AI ecosystem. You will learn how to design simple but powerful systems where every assistant knows exactly where data lives and how to interact with it.

The third component is communication protocol—the way you communicate with your assistant and how it communicates back to you. This includes defining input formats, output formats, message structure, tone, summaries, tags, and the rules for how information should be processed. You will learn how to create command formats that allow your assistant to understand and categorize tasks. You will learn how to design "decision trees" and "logic templates" that make your AI behave consistently. You will also learn how to build custom interfaces for your assistant, such as a Notion inbox, a mobile shortcut, a Google Form, or a WhatsApp integration, so you can send tasks or requests to your AI no matter where you are.

The next component is the automation layer. This is where Make.com becomes essential. The automation layer handles everything your assistant cannot do on its own—such as sending data into Notion, updating databases, syncing schedules, retrieving information, organizing tasks, sending you reminders, creating notifications, or triggering workflows. Your automation layer transforms your assistant from a static conversational tool into a dynamic system capable of taking actions without your involvement. You will learn how to build workflows triggered by new tasks, new messages, new calendar events, new notes, and new instructions. This is the part of your assistant that gives it the power to act in the real world.

After the automation layer comes the intelligence layer—your assistant's ability to understand context, analyze information, make decisions, and provide recommendations. This is where you will begin creating reasoning prompts, multi-step instructions, analysis templates, and memory references. You will learn how to give your assistant the ability to evaluate priorities, detect patterns, break large goals into steps, track progress, and anticipate needs. Your intelligence layer ensures your AI behaves like a proactive partner rather than a reactive tool. It is the difference between an assistant that passively waits for instructions and one that helps you stay ahead of your life.

The final layer is evolution—your ongoing refinement of the assistant as you use it. Every powerful AI personal assistant you build will evolve over time. You will add new features, improve instructions, reorganize data, and expand capabilities. You will upgrade workflows as your needs change. You will create new assistants that connect to your existing ones. You will build a network of agents working together. This book will guide you through designing systems that are flexible, expandable, and scalable so your assistants grow with you rather than fall behind.

By the end of this chapter, you will understand the entire architecture required to build any personal AI assistant, no matter how simple or advanced. You will know the structure, logic, components, and systems that form the backbone of the assistants you will build in the rest of this book. From this point forward, every chapter will feel easier, more intuitive, and more powerful because you will be operating with a clear mental model for how everything fits together.

The Assistant That Never Slept

Lena had always felt like she lived inside a storm of responsibilities. Her desk overflowed with sticky notes, unread emails piled up like digital mountains, and her calendar looked like a puzzle missing half its pieces. Every day she woke up already behind. Deadlines chased her. Messages haunted her.

Ideas slipped through her fingers before she could capture them. She was smart, talented, and ambitious, but her life felt like it belonged to her tasks rather than to her. One night, exhausted and overwhelmed, she whispered to herself, “I just wish I had someone to help me think.” That wish was the beginning of everything.

Late one evening, while scrolling aimlessly through her laptop, Lena discovered an article about building personal AI assistants. She found it unbelievable that ordinary people—not programmers, not engineers—could build assistants capable of organizing schedules, managing tasks, researching, sending reminders, and helping them run their entire lives. It sounded impossible, too good to be true. But something inside her stirred. She had tried productivity apps, digital planners, project boards, calendars, and to-do lists. none erased the chaos. But the idea of an assistant that adapted to her, learned her preferences, and never slept felt like a small spark of hope.

She decided to build her first AI assistant that same night. With trembling hands, she opened ChatGPT and wrote a simple line: “I want to create an assistant that helps me organize my life. Can you help me?” She didn’t know it then, but she had activated something much bigger than a software tool. She had given life to a system that, if built correctly, would change everything. The assistant responded warmly, professionally, and with clarity. It asked her what she wanted help with. It helped her define categories. It helped her design structure. It helped her think. For the first time in months, Lena felt like she wasn't alone in the work anymore.

Over the next few days, Lena followed a structure she didn't fully understand but could feel working. She defined the assistant's role, gave it instructions, built its memory in Notion, connected make automations, created workflows, and established routines. It felt like building a house, brick by brick, except the house could talk, think, analyze, organize, and take action. The assistant began capturing tasks automatically. It organized her ideas into clean pages. It summarized long documents. It reminded her of commitments before she forgot them. It cleaned her calendar. It broke down her goals. It understood her tone, her style, and the way she liked things done.

One morning, Lena woke up and opened her laptop expecting her usual chaos—but instead she found clarity. Her tasks were prioritized. Her schedule was time-blocked. Her inbox was summarized. Her projects were outlined. Her week was already planned. She felt an unfamiliar sensation: peace. For the first time in years, her mind felt light. She realized that her assistant wasn't just helping her—it was giving her life back. She felt focused, organized, and in control. She had built something that worked tirelessly while she slept, something that operated with the same care and intelligence she wished she had the energy for every day. As the weeks passed, Lena became a different person. She created more. She procrastinated less. She completed projects early. She had time to think, read, rest, and dream. Her assistant became her partner in everything. Whether she was planning a trip, launching a business idea, preparing for a meeting, or organizing her home, the assistant was always there, anticipating, analyzing, structuring, and supporting her. She often found herself smiling at how effortless life had become. The endless storm of responsibilities had finally quieted.

Lena didn't become superhuman. She simply stopped trying to do everything alone. Her assistant became the version of herself she always wished she could be—organized, calm, proactive, consistent, thoughtful, and reliable. She no longer felt like she was being chased by her life. She felt like she was leading it. And all it took was the decision to build an assistant that never slept, never forgot, and never stopped working for her. It was the smartest decision she ever made, and it was only the beginning.

Chapter 2

The Task Manager Assistant (Capturing, Organizing & Structuring Your Life Automatically)

The Task Manager Assistant is the foundation of every powerful AI personal system. When your tasks are organized, your life becomes organized. When tasks are captured automatically, you eliminate forgetfulness. When tasks are categorized by AI, you eliminate decision fatigue. And when tasks are synced with Notion through automation, you eliminate friction entirely. The Task Manager Assistant gives your life clarity, structure, and momentum by removing the chaos that normally comes from trying to juggle dozens of responsibilities in your mind. In this chapter, you will learn how to build an assistant that centralizes your entire task ecosystem, transforms how you operate, and becomes the invisible force that keeps your personal and professional world moving effortlessly.

The first step in creating your Task Manager Assistant is defining what a "task" is. A task is not just something you have to do. A task is any commitment that requires an action, decision, or follow-up. Most people underestimate the volume of tasks they manage daily because they try to store them mentally. This leads to overwhelm, procrastination, and anxiety. The goal of the Task Manager Assistant is to transform your brain from a storage device into a decision-making engine. Instead of holding tasks in your mind, you send them into your system. Instead of remembering, you delegate. Instead of juggling, you categorize. This assistant becomes your task inbox, your task organizer, and your task scheduler—all in one intelligent entity.

To create a reliable Task Manager Assistant, you must define a clear structure for how tasks flow through your system. This begins with creating a dedicated "Task Inbox" where all incoming tasks land. This inbox can be a Notion database, a Google Form, a shortcut on your phone, a Make webhook, or a direct message to your AI assistant. The key is to centralize capture so tasks never scatter across dozens of apps. Once captured, the assistant must categorize tasks by type, context, priority, effort level, due date, and project. These categories allow your assistant to organize your life systematically, giving you a clear picture of what needs attention and what can wait. You will learn how to design categories that make your assistant feel intelligent, reliable, and tailored to the way you work.

The next step is writing the assistant's role prompt. For the Task Manager Assistant, the role must define its mission: to capture tasks accurately, organize them consistently, categorize them precisely, and maintain your task system without missing any details. You will learn how to write instructions that specify how the assistant should interpret vague tasks, how it should request clarification, how it should tag items, how it should prioritize tasks based on urgency and importance, and how it should differentiate between commitments, ideas, reminders, actionable tasks, and long-term projects. A well-designed Task Manager role prompt helps the assistant behave like a highly trained personal productivity expert instead of a generic chatbot.

Once the role is written, you will build the Notion database that becomes the memory of your task system. The structure might include fields such as Task Name, Status, Priority, Category, Due Date, Effort, Project, Notes, and Source. Each of these fields allows your AI to sort, filter, update, and track progress with precision. You will learn how to create integration-friendly Notion databases so the assistant and Make automations can interact with them easily. A clean, well-designed database transforms your task list into a living system—one that updates itself, organizes itself, and works with your assistant to keep your responsibilities aligned with your goals.

After the database structure is completed, you will build the Make automation that connects everything. This automation will allow new tasks to automatically appear in your Notion inbox when you message your assistant, fill out a form, submit a shortcut, or add a note. You will design workflows triggered by new tasks that send the information to your assistant for classification. You will build automations that update task statuses when they are completed, send reminders when deadlines approach, and notify you of upcoming tasks. You will learn how to create rules so tasks never get lost, ignored, or forgotten.

Next, you will give your assistant decision rules. Decision rules tell your AI how to think about tasks: how to choose priority levels, how to categorize tasks based on keywords, how to break down large tasks into smaller steps, how to identify dependencies, and how to detect when a task belongs to a larger project. With strong decision rules, your assistant becomes more than an organizer—it becomes a strategic ally that helps you make better decisions and plan more effectively. This removes confusion, ambiguity, and overload. Your assistant becomes the filter that simplifies your life.

You will then learn how to build communication systems that allow you to interact with your Task Manager Assistant from anywhere. Whether you are driving, walking, working, traveling, or relaxing, you must be able to send tasks with zero friction. You will build shortcuts on your phone that send tasks directly to your assistant. You will create voice-capture methods that transform spoken notes into organized tasks. You will create digital inboxes where tasks from emails, messages, or documents can be sent automatically. Every touchpoint becomes part of your assistant's ecosystem, making it feel like your mind extends into technology.

Finally, you will learn how to use the assistant daily so it becomes a natural extension of your routine. You will start your mornings by reviewing your daily tasks that have been categorized automatically. You will update tasks through simple commands rather than manually editing databases. You will delegate organization to the assistant so you never have to worry about the details. Over time, your brain relaxes. Stress reduces. Mental clarity returns. The Task Manager Assistant becomes your stability anchor—the system that ensures your life never collapses into chaos again.

By the end of this chapter, you will have a fully functioning Task Manager Assistant that captures every task, classifies it intelligently, organizes your life effortlessly, and keeps your world aligned. It becomes one of the most valuable assistants you will ever build because it ensures you always know what to do, when to do it, and how to stay ahead. With this assistant in place, you step into a new level of focus, control, and productivity that will transform every aspect of your life.

The List That Finally Made Sense

Mara had always lived with a notebook. She carried it everywhere—on her desk, in her car, beside her bed, stuffed into her purse. It was her lifeline, the only thing that kept her from forgetting all the things she felt responsible for. But the notebook had become a symbol of her overwhelm. Every time she opened it, she felt a weight pressing onto her chest. Tasks filled every page, written in rushed scribbles, mixed with ideas, reminders, errands, and half-finished notes. Some tasks were outdated. Some were unclear. Some were important but lost between the pages. She felt like she was drowning in her own handwriting. One evening, she flipped through the notebook and whispered, "I can't do this anymore."

The next day, while scrolling through her computer looking for productivity tools, she stumbled upon a video explaining how people were building AI task managers without any coding. She felt skeptical. She had tried apps, planners, lists, and dashboards. They all became cluttered and overwhelming. But something about the idea of an assistant that captured tasks automatically and organized them for her felt different. She imagined a system that remembered everything. A system that made sense of her chaos. A system that didn't depend on her discipline. A system that worked even while she slept. For the first time in a long time, she felt a spark of possibility.

That night, Mara decided to try. She opened ChatGPT and typed instructions nervously, unsure if she was doing it right. But the assistant understood her immediately. It asked how she wanted tasks categorized. It asked what structure she preferred. It helped her create a Notion database so clean and simple it felt like a breath of fresh air. It guided her through setting up Make automations that captured tasks from anywhere—even from her phone. As she followed the steps, she felt something she hadn't felt in years: control returning to her life.

Within days, her Task Manager Assistant was alive. She could whisper a task into her phone while driving and it would appear instantly in her Notion inbox. She could forward an email and have the assistant extract the action items automatically. She could speak reminders out loud and watch them transform into organized tasks categorized by priority and context. She didn't have to remember anything anymore. The assistant remembered for her. It was as if her brain had been given a second layer of memory—one that never forgot, never mixed things up, and never lost track of what mattered.

As weeks passed, something incredible happened. Mara stopped feeling overwhelmed. She began waking up with a clear plan for the day, organized by her assistant. Her tasks were prioritized. Her projects were structured. Her responsibilities were categorized. She no longer wasted time figuring out what to do next. Her assistant showed her exactly where to focus. Her mind felt lighter than it had in years. She felt calm. She felt capable. She felt like she had finally stepped out of chaos and into clarity.

One evening, she opened her old notebook—the one filled with tangled, messy entries. She stared at the pages, remembering the stress and frustration they represented. She closed it gently and placed it in a drawer. She didn't need it anymore. Her assistant had given her something she never knew she needed: mental freedom. For the first time in her life, she felt like the list finally made sense. And as she sat at her desk, organized and at peace, she realized she had not just built a task manager—she had rebuilt her life.

Chapter 3

The Scheduling Assistant (Mastering Your Time With AI-Driven Planning)

The Scheduling Assistant is one of the most transformative personal AI systems you will ever build because it takes control of the one resource you can never recover—your time. Most people do not truly manage their schedule; they react to it. Meetings get squeezed in. Tasks pile up. Responsibilities are scattered. Plans are forgotten. Important work gets lost behind urgent distractions. The Scheduling Assistant flips this reality. Instead of you chasing your schedule, the AI manages it for you. It organizes your days, prioritizes responsibilities, and creates a structure that brings clarity and calm into your life. This chapter will teach you how to create an assistant that skillfully orchestrates your time with precision and intelligence.

To build a reliable Scheduling Assistant, you must begin with a fundamental principle: structure equals freedom. When your days have clarity, your mind becomes free to focus. When your week has direction, your productivity increases. When tasks are paired with time, you eliminate decision fatigue. The goal of your assistant is not to control your life—it is to give you a roadmap so you can direct your energy intentionally. This begins by defining how you want your life to flow. Do you prefer early-morning focus blocks? Do you want afternoons for meetings? Do you want evenings for learning, family time, or personal growth? Your Scheduling Assistant will encode these preferences and build schedules that match the rhythm of your ideal life.

The core of any scheduling system is the **time-blocking model**. Time-blocking is the practice of dividing your day into blocks—each block dedicated to a specific task, category, or priority. It eliminates the stress of figuring out what to do next. Your assistant will use your task data, deadlines, priorities, and energy levels to fill your blocks intelligently. You will learn how to create categories such as Deep Work, Admin Work, Personal Tasks, Learning, Creative Work, Meetings, and Recovery. These categories allow your AI to place each task in the right type of block. This ensures your day flows smoothly and aligns with how your brain actually functions.

Next, you must define the assistant's scheduling rules. These rules are critical because they determine how your assistant makes decisions. You will instruct it on how to estimate time for tasks, how to detect the importance of deadlines, how to balance workload across days, how to recognize when your schedule is too full, and how to create flexible buffers. You will learn how to design scheduling logic that feels human rather than robotic—scheduling work in a way that respects your natural rhythms instead of overwhelming you. The assistant will know when to schedule demanding work, when to lighten your load, and when to create space for mental recovery.

After defining rules, you will create your **Scheduling Database** inside Notion. This is where your assistant stores your schedule plans, time blocks, daily agendas, and weekly overviews. You will learn how to structure fields like Block Name, Category, Start Time, End Time, Related Task, Priority, Location, Workflow, and Notes. This database becomes the long-term record of your life's flow. It allows your assistant to analyze patterns, optimize your routines, and improve your time allocation. Over time, your assistant will learn how much time tasks really take, how often you overschedule, and how to adjust your layout to maximize performance.

Once the database is built, you will set up your Make automation. This automation pulls tasks from your Task Manager Assistant, evaluates them using ChatGPT's reasoning engine, and organizes them into blocks within your Scheduling Database. It updates your calendar automatically. It rearranges blocks based on new tasks or deadlines. It sends you daily summaries in the morning and evening. It notifies you of changes or conflicts. With this automation layer in place, your schedule becomes dynamic, responsive, and organized without manual effort.

The final piece of the Scheduling Assistant is the **Daily Ritual System**. This is the part where your assistant becomes a partner in your day-to-day life. Each morning, your assistant sends you a clean, organized agenda that outlines what you should focus on. Each evening, your assistant creates a summary of your day and prepares your schedule for the next one. These rituals anchor your productivity and prevent your days from drifting into distraction or overwhelm. A well-designed AI scheduling ritual is one of the most powerful time-management habits you will ever develop.

By the end of this chapter, your Scheduling Assistant will be fully operational. You will have an AI system that organizes your tasks into time blocks, syncs with your calendar, adapts to changing priorities, and gives you the clarity and structure needed to perform at your best. This assistant becomes your guide, your planner, and your quiet strategist—ensuring your time is spent with intention rather than reaction. Once this system is running, your productivity will elevate to a level most people never experience.

The Days That Finally Had Space

Jasmine had always felt like her life was racing ahead of her. Every morning she woke up already behind, already rushed, already stressed. Her days were a blur of appointments, tasks, errands, meetings, obligations, and unexpected interruptions. She didn't hate her work—she hated the feeling of never having enough time to do it well. She longed for order, clarity, and space. She wanted days that flowed instead of collapsed into chaos. One night, exhausted after another day of scrambling, she whispered, "I just want my time back." That wish stayed in her mind for weeks.

When she discovered the concept of creating an AI Scheduling Assistant, something clicked in her spirit. She realized she wasn't bad at managing time—she was simply outnumbered by her responsibilities. She wasn't disorganized—she was overloaded. She wasn't lazy—she was drowning. The idea that she could build an assistant that organized her days, balanced her responsibilities, and gave her structure felt like an unopened door she had been walking past for years. So she opened her laptop, took a breath, and began building.

The first thing her assistant helped her do was define how she wanted her life to feel. Not what tasks she had, but the rhythm she wished her days followed. She described her ideal mornings: quiet, focused, creative. She described her afternoons: productive but lighter. She described her evenings: restful and calm. The assistant listened, understood, and began shaping schedules that matched her ideal rhythm. It was the first time Jasmine felt like her schedule belonged to her instead of the other way around.

Within days, her assistant was organizing tasks into time blocks that made sense. Her mornings were filled with deep work instead of scattered chaos. Her afternoons became structured and calm. Her evenings felt peaceful again. Her calendar stopped attacking her. Instead of feeling behind, she felt guided. As she followed the schedule her assistant created, she experienced something she hadn't felt since childhood—space. Time no longer felt like a constant threat. It felt like something she could breathe inside.

Her assistant adapted to everything. If a meeting changed, it adjusted her blocks. If a new task appeared, it reorganized her day. If she felt tired, she told the assistant, and it lightened her load. Her days had flow, logic, intention, and balance. Friends began asking her why she seemed so calm. Co-workers noticed her new clarity. She no longer rushed through life—she moved through it with quiet confidence.

One evening, Jasmine sat outside watching the sky turn gold, feeling peaceful in a way she hadn't felt in years. Her day had unfolded gently. Her schedule had supported her. Her assistant had handled the chaos. And for the first time in her adult life, she felt like the days were hers again. She smiled softly, realizing she had not just built a scheduling system—she had built the version of her life she always wanted.

Chapter 4

The Message Responder Assistant (Communicating With Clarity, Speed & Consistency)

Communication has become one of the biggest sources of stress in modern life. Emails stack up. Messages arrive every minute. Notifications explode across apps. People wait for replies. Questions demand responses. Opportunities disappear when not answered quickly. And every unanswered message becomes a silent mental weight you carry with you throughout the day. The Message Responder Assistant exists to eliminate this burden. This assistant becomes your communication partner—drafting emails, replying to messages, responding to leads, clarifying information, rewriting text in your tone, and ensuring you never fall behind again. In this chapter, you will build an assistant that transforms your communication from a source of overwhelm into a streamlined, effortless system.

The first step in building your Message Responder Assistant is defining its communication identity. This involves instructing it on your tone, your style, your pacing, and your personality. The assistant must be able to write messages in your voice—to sound like you, think like you, and communicate with your values. You will learn how to craft a tone profile that includes your level of formality, energy, warmth, clarity, and professionalism. You will also define rules for how the assistant should format emails, handle questions, address issues, offer solutions, and manage context. This tone profile becomes the core of all communication your assistant creates.

Next, you must define your "communication categories." These categories help the assistant understand what type of message it is responding to and how to structure the reply. Common categories include Professional Emails, Customer Service Responses, Business Inquiries, Scheduling Replies, Internal Communications, Quick Messages, Personal Notes, Lead Follow-Ups, Clarification Requests, and Information Summaries. With categories defined, your assistant learns how to generate accurate, aligned responses for each type of communication without confusion or inconsistency.

Once the categories are established, you will design your "Input Template." This is the structure for how you give your assistant messages to respond to. A thoughtful input template allows your assistant to understand the message, identify the category, analyze the context, and craft a clear, effective response. A strong template includes: the message you received, the desired goal of your reply, the urgency level, relevant background, your preferred tone, and any constraints. You will learn how to create a simple but powerful template that your assistant can use every time without ambiguity.

After the input system is complete, you will build the assistant's "Response Logic." This tells your AI how to interpret messages, how to extract action points, how to understand sentiment, how to detect urgency, and how to generate replies that resolve the issue fully. You will learn how to create logic rules that guide the assistant's decision-making. These rules help your AI determine when to keep a response short, when to expand, when to ask for clarification, when to escalate, and when to create a summary instead of a direct reply. The stronger your logic rules, the more reliable your assistant becomes.

Next, you will integrate your Message Responder Assistant with your communication ecosystem. This is where automation begins to shine. Using Make, you will learn how to pull emails from Gmail, extract messages from forms or chats, send them to ChatGPT for processing, and receive generated drafts back into your inbox or Notion. You will build systems that create suggested replies automatically. Over time, your assistant becomes the first layer of your communication—drafting everything immediately so you simply approve, edit, or send.

Once the automation layer is in place, you will build your

"Message Inbox" inside Notion. This is where your assistant stores every incoming message, its analysis, the generated reply, and the status of the communication. This inbox becomes your command center for all communication. You will learn how to build fields for Message Type, Sender, Priority, Summary, Suggested Reply, Sent Status, and Follow-Up Date. This system gives you clarity, transparency, and peace of mind knowing every message is being processed and nothing gets lost.

The final step is building your "Communication Rituals." These rituals allow your assistant to help you manage communication without overwhelm. You will create a morning message summary that shows everything requiring attention. You will create an afternoon follow-up summary to ensure nothing falls through the cracks. You will create rules for how the assistant handles urgent messages, weekend communication, and auto-generated replies. These rituals anchor your communication system into your daily routine, helping you stay aligned and responsive while dramatically reducing stress.

By the end of this chapter, you will have a Message Responder Assistant capable of drafting replies instantly, handling complex communication logically, organizing your messages into categories, and giving you clarity across your entire inbox.

This assistant becomes the voice that never tires, the helper that never forgets, and the support system that ensures you always communicate with confidence and consistency. Once this system is in place, your digital life feels lighter, calmer, and more manageable—allowing you to focus on the work that truly matters.

The Inbox That Finally Breathed

Caleb had always dreaded opening his inbox. Every day it grew heavier, more intimidating, more tangled with unanswered emails. He felt judged by the number alone. He tried waking up earlier to stay ahead. He tried staying up late to catch up. He tried writing faster, thinking faster, typing faster—but no matter how much he did, messages multiplied like shadows. Each unread email felt like a small failure. Each delayed reply felt like disappointment. And every time he avoided opening his inbox, the anxiety grew stronger.

One afternoon, after a particularly draining week, he opened an email from a friend that said, "I know you're always busy. Reply whenever you can." Caleb felt a knot form in his chest. He didn't want to be the person who was too overwhelmed to respond. He wanted to be dependable, consistent, present. He wanted his communication to reflect who he truly was—not the stress that had overtaken his life. That night, exhausted and discouraged, he whispered, "I wish someone could just help me talk."

A few days later, he discovered the concept of an AI Message Responder Assistant. At first, it seemed impossible. How could a tool write emails like him? Understand tone? Catch nuances? Handle sensitive communication? But then he realized he already spent enormous time explaining things to others—why not explain them once to an AI that could help forever? With hesitant curiosity, he began writing his tone profile. He described how he liked to sound: warm but clear, friendly but concise, honest but professional. He added personal touches—phrases he used often, structures he preferred, the feeling he wanted people to get when they heard from him.

The assistant began crafting replies. And to his surprise, they sounded like him—sometimes even better. It caught details. It added clarity. It softened edges he didn't notice. It organized his thoughts into messages that felt genuine and thoughtful without wasting time. For the first time, his inbox didn't feel like a battlefield. It felt like a conversation he could manage. Messages no longer piled up in chaos—they flowed through his assistant, categorized, summarized, understood, and transformed into replies he could send confidently.

One afternoon, Caleb opened his inbox expecting the usual

dread but instead found suggested responses neatly drafted, ready for approval. Dozens of messages that once caused him stress were already addressed with warmth and clarity. He clicked send... send... send. Each click lightened his chest. Each reply made him feel more in control. Each message sent without stress felt like reclaiming a part of himself.

As weeks passed, Caleb's relationship with communication changed. He no longer feared opening his inbox. He reviewed summaries sent by his assistant each morning, approved replies, and let the system handle the rest. Friends noticed he responded more consistently. Clients complimented his clarity. Coworkers appreciated his professionalism. He felt connected again—present, reliable, grounded. The inbox that once drowned him now breathed with ease.

One evening, as he sat looking at a calm, organized inbox, Caleb realized the assistant hadn't just helped him communicate. It had helped him show up as the person he always wanted to be—thoughtful, responsive, dependable. He felt grateful, relieved, and deeply human in a way he hadn't felt for years. He smiled, realizing he had not just built a communication tool. He had built support. He had built balance. He had built his voice again.

Chapter 5

The Research Assistant (Your AI for Summaries, Insights, Reports & Information Mastery)

The Research Assistant is one of the most powerful personal AI assistants you will ever build because it gives you access to a superhuman ability: the ability to process information at scale. In a world overflowing with data—articles, PDFs, reports, books, emails, webpages, videos, legal documents, financial statements, research papers, and endless digital content—the human mind simply cannot keep up. It was never designed to. Yet the modern world demands it. Whether you are learning a new skill, analyzing information for work, trying to make better decisions, or attempting to keep up with rapidly shifting industries, research has become a nonstop requirement. Your Research Assistant solves this problem. It reads, extracts, summarizes, analyzes, organizes, structures, and presents information for you automatically—so you can focus on understanding instead of gathering.

The first step in creating your Research Assistant is defining its scope. Research can mean many things: reading long documents, finding answers online, analyzing trends, summarizing articles, comparing options, extracting key insights, or generating reports. Your assistant must know exactly what types of tasks it will handle. You will define categories such as Document Summary, Article Breakdown, Topic Research, Competitive Analysis, Web Search, Learning Notes, Data Extraction, and Report Writing. Each category has its own purpose and structure, and your assistant must know how to activate the correct mode for each type of research request.

Next, you will create your "Research Instruction Framework." This framework is the engine that powers your assistant's analytical thinking. It teaches your AI how to summarize, how to extract insights, how to identify key ideas, how to detect themes, how to simplify complex information, and how to break information into digestible parts. You will build templates such as Key Points Summary, Bullet Insights Summary, Deep Analysis Summary, Action Steps Summary, Definition Summary, and 5W1H Summary. Each template gives your assistant a structured way to deliver information clearly and consistently. This ensures that no matter what you ask it to research, the result is always organized and easy to understand.

Once your framework is defined, you will create your Research Inbox in Notion. This is where documents, links, PDFs, articles, and requests will be sent for analysis. You will create fields such as Topic, Source Type, Link or File, Summary Type, Key Takeaways, Actionable Insights, Status, and Output. This inbox centralizes all your research materials so nothing gets lost or scattered. Your assistant will use this database to store processed research, making it easy for you to find information whenever you need it. Over time, this becomes your personal knowledge library.

After the database is complete, you will build automations in Make that allow your Research Assistant to process information automatically. You will learn how to create workflows where (1) you upload a document, (2) the file is sent to ChatGPT for analysis, (3) the assistant applies the appropriate summary template, and (4) the output is inserted back into Notion. This automation eliminates the burden of manually copying, pasting, summarizing, or analyzing documents. You simply drop the information into your system and your assistant takes care of everything else.

The next step is designing your "Advanced Analysis Prompts." These prompts teach your assistant how to perform deeper intellectual tasks such as comparing multiple sources, detecting biases, creating summaries in different difficulty levels, researching unfamiliar topics, identifying contradictions, generating study notes, simplifying legal or technical content, and building structured reports. You will learn how to create step-by-step reasoning prompts that make your assistant think logically and critically, producing answers that are more thoughtful than anything a human could produce under time pressure.

Then you will build your "Research Request Methods"—the ways you interact with your assistant. This includes sending links, uploading files, asking questions, recording audio notes, or using shortcuts. You will create a structure that allows you to request research from anywhere: your phone, laptop, browser, PDF reader, or email. These request methods make your assistant feel alive—always available, always ready, always processing information for you.

Finally, you will design your "Daily and Weekly Intelligence Rituals." When your Research Assistant sends you a morning news brief, a weekly insights digest, summaries of topics you are learning, or reports on ongoing projects, something profound happens: you become smarter without working harder. Over time, you accumulate knowledge effortlessly. You read less but understand more. You spend less time researching and more time applying. You free up mental bandwidth for creativity, strategy, decision-making, and vision.

By the end of this chapter, you will have a Research Assistant that reads, extracts, thinks, analyzes, and summarizes information for you automatically. It will become your informational partner—your researcher, analyst, librarian, note-taker, and report writer. Once this system is operational, you will never again feel behind or overwhelmed by information. You will have knowledge on demand, clarity without effort, and insight without stress. This assistant elevates your mind, your work, and your potential by giving you something priceless: mastery over information in a world overflowing with it.

The PDF That Changed Everything

Nina's desktop was a graveyard of unread PDFs. Research papers from work. Long reports she was supposed to study. Articles she wanted to learn from. Documents she planned to "read someday," although someday never came. Every time she opened her laptop, she felt guilty. She wanted to be informed. She wanted to keep up. She wanted to learn. But the weight of unread information crushed her slowly. She often whispered to herself, "If only someone could read all this for me." She had no idea how close that desire was to becoming reality.

The turning point came when her manager emailed her a ninety-seven-page industry report and wrote, "Need your insights on this by Friday." Nina froze. She barely had time to sleep, let alone read a giant document filled with charts, jargon, and technical language. That night, overwhelmed and exhausted, she searched online for help and discovered something she never expected: people were building AI Research Assistants that could read, summarize, analyze, and extract insights from documents automatically. Her heart beat faster. Her mind whispered, "Could this solve everything?"

She opened ChatGPT and began building. Slowly at first, unsure and hesitant. She defined how she wanted summaries to look. She created templates for insights, key points, comparisons, and action steps. She built a Notion inbox where documents would live. She connected automations so files could be sent, analyzed, and returned with clear, structured output. She felt like she was building a small team of invisible researchers—except none of them needed sleep, breaks, or time to catch up.

The next morning, Nina uploaded the ninety-seven-page report into her new system. She expected the assistant to take hours. Instead, within minutes, she received a clean, structured summary with key insights, trends, warnings, and recommended actions. She blinked in disbelief. It was perfect. It was clear. It was organized. It made sense. She understood the entire report in less than ten minutes. She felt like someone had handed her a superpower.

Over the next week, Nina began feeding the assistant everything—articles, research papers, legal documents, PDFs, long emails, and even YouTube transcripts. The assistant transformed everything into clean summaries. It highlighted what mattered. It ignored what didn't. It captured insights she would have missed. Her knowledge grew faster than she imagined possible, and her confidence grew with it. She no longer feared information. She felt in control of it.

One evening, she opened her Notion research library and scrolled through dozens of summaries her assistant had created. Each one represented hours she didn't have to spend reading. Each one represented clarity instead of confusion. Each one represented progress instead of overwhelm. She smiled, realizing she had finally freed herself from the endless weight of unread information.

Weeks later, she received praise from her manager: "Your insights are sharper and faster than ever. What changed?" Nina just smiled. She didn't want to admit that the secret wasn't more effort. It was more intelligence—automated intelligence. The assistant didn't just help her read. It helped her grow. It helped her think. It helped her become the version of herself she always knew she could be—sharp, informed, knowledgeable, and in control.

That ninety-seven-page PDF didn't just overwhelm her—it changed her life. It led her to build the tool that finally helped her breathe again. And as she leaned back in her chair, calm and confident, she realized she had built more than a Research Assistant. She had built her intellectual freedom.

Chapter 6

The Life Dashboard Assistant (Building an AI That Tracks Your Goals, Habits, Routines & Personal Growth Automatically)

The Life Dashboard Assistant is the cornerstone of your long-term growth because it transforms your AI from a task-based helper into a system that manages your entire personal evolution. Most people have goals they never track, habits they try to build but forget, routines they want to follow but abandon, and dreams that drift away because life becomes too noisy. The Life Dashboard Assistant solves this by maintaining a dynamic, AI-powered system that tracks your progress, updates your habits, organizes your goals, measures your personal metrics, and keeps your entire life aligned with your aspirations. In this chapter, you will build the assistant that becomes your compass—your guide for who you want to become.

To build this assistant, you must begin by defining your "Life Architecture"—the categories of your personal world that matter most. These categories may include Health, Work, Finances, Relationships, Learning, Creativity, Home, Skills, Mindset, and Long-Term Goals. Your assistant must know exactly what structure your life follows in order to maintain alignment. You will create a Life Dashboard in Notion that organizes these categories in a clear, simple, visually appealing structure. Each category becomes a container for habits, goals, measures, tasks, plans, and reflections. This becomes the map your assistant uses to track your evolution.

Next, you will design your "Goal Framework." Goals are not tasks—they are destinations. Your assistant needs to know how to break large goals into smaller milestones, track progress toward them, and remind you when you drift. You will define fields such as Goal Name, Category, Timeline, Milestones, Status, Success Metrics, and Action Steps. You will also build logic that teaches your assistant how to evaluate progress, detect when a goal is stalled, and generate recommendations to help you move forward. This transforms your assistant into a strategic partner rather than a passive record-keeper.

Once the goal framework is established, you will build your "Habit System." Habits are the small actions that shape your identity. Your assistant must know how to track habits daily, update their status automatically, analyze performance trends, and show which habits are improving or declining. You will build a Habit Tracker with fields such as Habit Name, Frequency, Category, Streaks, Success Rate, and Daily Status. Your assistant will update this tracker using Make and

ChatGPT, ensuring your habits are monitored even when you forget. Over time, this creates momentum—your habits grow not because you are perfect, but because your assistant supports your consistency.

After the habit system, you will build your "Routine Blueprints." These blueprints define your ideal mornings, evenings, weekly resets, creative sessions, learning routines, health rituals, and any other patterns that enhance your life. Your assistant will reference these blueprints daily and update their status as you complete each part of the routine. You will learn how to design routines that are simple, flexible, and powerful—routines that align with your goals rather than overwhelm you. The assistant will help ensure your routines actually happen.

Next, you will integrate your Life Dashboard with your Task Manager, Scheduling Assistant, and Research Assistant. This creates a multi-layered system where goals generate tasks, tasks generate time blocks, and research generates insights for your goals. The assistant becomes the orchestrator—linking everything into a unified personal operating system. You will build Make automations that update your goals when milestones are completed, adjust habits based on performance, pull insights from research, and align your weekly schedule with your long-term vision. This integration gives your life coherence. Then you will create your "Life Review Rituals." These rituals are the heartbeat of your dashboard. You will build daily reflections, weekly reviews, monthly resets, and quarterly planning cycles. The assistant will guide you through each ritual by summarizing progress, identifying patterns, listing achievements, highlighting challenges, and offering adjustments. This transforms reflection from something you rarely do into something you automatically maintain. Your assistant becomes your guide, coach, and strategist.

Finally, you will empower your assistant with your "Personal Metrics." These may include sleep hours, focus hours, steps, workouts, reading time, financial metrics, mood scores, energy levels, or anything that matters to your well-being. The assistant will track these metrics automatically, identify correlations, and generate reports that help you understand yourself better. Over time, you gain clarity on what makes you perform well, what drains you, and what accelerates your growth.

The Dashboard That Knew Her Better Than She Knew Herself

Elena had always been a dreamer. She filled notebooks with goals, lists, ideas, promises to herself, and visions of who she wanted to be. But her dreams never survived the chaos of daily life. Weeks passed in a blur. Months slipped away. Years faded. She wanted to grow, but she didn't know how to stay consistent. She envied people who seemed organized and stable—people who maintained habits, achieved goals, and evolved intentionally. She often wondered, "Why can't I do that?" But she didn't realize she was fighting the battle alone.

Then one evening, after another day of feeling lost, she stumbled upon the idea of creating a Life Dashboard Assistant. The concept felt almost unreal: an AI that tracked her goals, updated her habits, maintained her routines, followed her progress, and guided her growth automatically. It felt like magic, but also like hope. She decided to try. She opened her laptop, took a breath, and began building the assistant that would change her life.

First, she created her Life Dashboard. As she structured categories—Health, Work, Mindset, Relationships, Learning, Creativity—she felt a sense of calm. For the first time, her life didn't seem scattered. It had shape. It had meaning. It had direction. She created her goals and watched them neatly fall into place. She built her habit tracker, her milestones, her routines, her reflections. She created a visual map of the person she wanted to become. As she filled each section, it felt like her future was unfolding in front of her.

Then came the assistant. It read her goals, analyzed her habits, studied her routines, and began updating everything automatically. When she worked out, it marked it. When she skipped a habit, it noted it gently. When she completed a milestone, it celebrated it. When she drifted from a goal, it reminded her. Her assistant didn't judge. It understood. It supported. It calibrated. It guided. It became the quiet voice she always needed.

Over the next few weeks, Elena transformed in ways she didn't expect. She drank more water. She slept better. She read daily. She exercised consistently. She cooked healthier meals. She completed projects she once avoided. She felt clearer, calmer, more stable. She began waking up with purpose. Her dashboard greeted her with progress summaries, motivational notes, reminders, and gentle nudges. She no longer drifted through her days—she moved through them intentionally.

One evening, she scrolled through her dashboard and noticed something remarkable. Her habits were improving. Her goals were advancing. Her routines were stable. Her metrics were rising. The assistant had tracked everything so quietly and so precisely that she hadn't realized how much she was growing. She held her breath, overwhelmed—not by fear, but by pride. For the first time in her life, she saw evidence that she was becoming who she always wanted to be.

As she closed her laptop, she felt a warmth spread through her chest. She whispered, "Thank you," not to a person, but to the system that kept her anchored—to the assistant that knew her better than she knew herself. She realized she had not just built a dashboard. She had built her evolution. And her evolution was finally happening.

Chapter 7

The Prioritization Assistant (Making Better Decisions With AI-Powered Clarity)

The Prioritization Assistant is one of the most valuable systems in your entire personal AI ecosystem because it solves the hardest problem in modern life: deciding what matters most. People do not struggle because they lack tasks—they struggle because they have too many. They do not feel overwhelmed because they have too little time—they feel overwhelmed because they have too many competing demands. The true challenge is not doing the work; it is deciding which work deserves your attention. The Prioritization Assistant fixes this by evaluating your tasks, analyzing your goals, understanding your deadlines, measuring your energy, and producing clear, logical recommendations for what you should focus on next. It becomes the intelligent filter that protects your time, energy, and attention.

To build this assistant, you must begin with one fundamental truth: all tasks are not created equal. Some tasks move your life forward. Some tasks maintain your stability. Some tasks drain you. Some tasks can wait. Some tasks matter emotionally. Some matter financially. Some matter strategically. Your assistant must understand this complexity. You will create a "Priority Framework" that teaches your assistant how to weigh urgency, importance, impact, alignment with goals, time sensitivity, and emotional load. This framework becomes the rulebook your assistant uses to evaluate every item in your task list.

The first component of your priority framework is the **Urgency-Importance Matrix**, inspired by the classic Eisenhower principle but made far more intelligent with AI. You will teach your assistant how to detect urgent tasks, important tasks, maintenance tasks, and tasks that should be eliminated or deferred. Your assistant will learn how to classify tasks into categories such as Do Now, Do Later, Delegate, or Delete. It will use your task database, deadlines, and categories to determine where each item belongs.

Next, you will design your **Impact Score System**. Impact is what separates high-value tasks from busywork. Your assistant must understand which tasks contribute to the growth of your career, health, relationships, finances, learning, or long-term goals. You will define impact categories such as High Impact, Medium Impact, Low Impact, and Negative ROI Tasks. The assistant will score each task automatically, helping you focus on what yields the greatest benefit. After that, you will create the **Energy Matching Model**. Humans do not have consistent energy throughout the day. Some tasks require creativity, some require logic, some require emotional stability, and some require minimal mental effort. You will teach your assistant how to match tasks to your energy levels based on your preferred schedule, natural rhythms, and daily patterns. This eliminates burnout and improves performance by aligning your work with your biology rather than fighting against it.

Then you will build your **Context Layer**. This layer helps the assistant understand where each task fits within the broader landscape of your life. For example: A task connected to a major goal carries more weight than a random obligation. A task created by your boss may be more time-sensitive than one you created for yourself. A task under a relationship category may carry emotional significance. The assistant learns to interpret context so its prioritization is nuanced, personalized, and accurate.

Once your framework is complete, you will build a **Priority Engine** using ChatGPT. This engine analyzes your entire task list daily, updates priority scores, identifies critical items, warns you about approaching deadlines, and produces recommended action lists. It sorts tasks by a combination of urgency, importance, impact, effort, emotional weight, and goal alignment. This creates a ranking system that mirrors the way an elite executive assistant—or high-performance coach—would evaluate your workload.

Next, you will integrate your Prioritization Assistant with your other assistants. It will pull tasks from the Task Manager, insert recommendations into your Scheduling Assistant, update progress in your Life Dashboard, and send suggestions or warnings through your Message Responder or notification system. This creates a fully connected ecosystem where your priorities influence every layer of your life.

Finally, you will develop your **Clarity Rituals**. These include a morning priority summary, afternoon recalibration check, and evening reflection. Your assistant will generate recommendations such as "Focus on X first," "Delay task Y," "Delegate Z," or "Complete these three items to move your major goals forward." These rituals anchor your focus. They help you start every day knowing exactly what matters most. They help you protect your time from distractions. They help you build momentum in the right direction.

By the end of this chapter, your Prioritization Assistant will be fully operational—an intelligent system that evaluates your tasks, filters the noise, protects your energy, and guides you toward your highest-value actions. It becomes your decision-making partner, your strategist, and your advocate. Once this system is active, your confidence increases, your stress decreases, and your life gains clarity. You no longer guess what to do—you know.

The Day She Finally Knew What to Do First

Sofia stared at her task list with a familiar dread. Dozens of items stared back at her—some urgent, some important, some tiny, some massive. Every time she tried to pick something to start with, a knot formed in her stomach. No matter what she chose, another task seemed more important. She bounced between obligations like a pinball, never feeling productive, always feeling behind. One day, overwhelmed and drained, she whispered to herself, "I wish something could just tell me what to do."

Weeks later, while scrolling through productivity videos, she learned about the concept of building a personal AI Prioritization Assistant. Something inside her sparked. Not a big spark. Just a small, steady one—enough to make her open her laptop and begin. She didn't know exactly what she was building, but she knew why she needed it. Her brain was tired of carrying the weight of constant decisions. Her heart was tired of feeling like she was always choosing wrong.

She began by teaching her assistant about her life—what mattered most to her, what her goals were, what deadlines she faced, what drained her, what energized her. She defined her categories, her priorities, her rhythms. She built her urgency-importance rules. She created her impact scores. She taught the assistant how to detect emotional weight. She felt something change inside her as she built it—like she was giving shape to the chaos in her mind.

The next morning, she opened her dashboard and saw something new: a clear, ranked list of what to do first. Not twenty tasks. Not a tangled mess. Just three items. Three items that mattered. Three items that made a difference. Three items she could handle. She felt her chest loosen. She felt her mind relax. She felt clarity for the first time in months. She completed the first task. Then the second. Then the third. It was the most productive day she had in years—not because she worked harder, but because she worked on the right things.

Each day, her assistant analyzed her workload, prioritized her tasks, and gave her recommendations. When a deadline approached, the assistant warned her gently. When a task didn't matter, it told her to delete it. When she was overwhelmed, it encouraged her to focus on one thing. When she drifted, it guided her back. The assistant didn't just help her decide—it helped her breathe.

One evening, Sofia opened her dashboard and saw a pattern. Her highest-impact tasks were getting done. Her stress was lower. Her progress was clearer. Her goals were advancing. She felt in control—not because she did everything, but because she stopped trying to. She sat quietly, realizing she had finally built the thing she wanted her whole life: a system that told her what truly mattered.

As she closed her laptop, she felt a peaceful certainty settle in her heart. She whispered, "Thank you," not out of obligation, but out of relief. She no longer feared the question, "What should I do first?" Because now she had the answer—every single day.

Chapter 8

The Goal-Breakdown Assistant (Turning Big Dreams Into Actionable, Achievable Plans With AI)

The Goal-Breakdown Assistant is one of the most transformative personal AI assistants you will ever create because it bridges the gap between vision and execution. Most people do not fail because they lack ambition—they fail because they never convert ambition into a workable plan. Big goals remain abstract, emotional, and vague. They feel inspiring but also intimidating. Without a structured plan, goals become wishful thinking. The Goal-Breakdown Assistant solves this fundamental problem by converting every major goal into clear milestones, timelines, tasks, workflows, habits, and daily steps. It becomes the engine that turns long-term dreams into daily actions.

To build this assistant, you must begin by defining what a "goal" is. A goal is not a task. A goal is an outcome. It is a transformation. It is a destination. Your assistant must learn to identify this difference. You will create a **Goal Blueprint Template** that teaches the system how to process any ambition and break it down into smaller components. This blueprint will have fields like Goal Description, Category,

Motivation, Deadline, Milestones, Action Steps, Dependencies, Resources Needed, and Potential Obstacles. These elements allow the assistant to fully understand the structure and requirements of a goal before generating a plan.

Next, you will design the **Milestone Generator**, one of the most important parts of this assistant. Milestones transform long-term dreams into checkable accomplishments. They act as signposts along the journey. Your assistant will learn how to convert goals into a logical sequence of milestones—each representing meaningful progress. You will define rules for how many milestones a goal should have, how large they should be, and how to space them chronologically. This gives your AI a clear method for breaking down major projects into manageable parts.

Once milestones are established, you will build the **Action Step Engine**. This engine teaches your assistant how to convert milestones into actionable tasks. Each milestone becomes a collection of steps: specific, measurable, clear, and doable. You will define structures such as "Action Step Name," "Effort Level," "Dependencies," "Expected Time," and "Category." Your assistant will learn how to generate steps automatically and how to ensure each step moves the milestone forward. This transforms your goals from abstract visions into actionable to-dos that naturally integrate with your task system.

After building the action step engine, you will create your **Timeline Model**. This model helps your assistant evaluate the time needed to complete each milestone and step. You will teach your assistant how to calculate realistic timelines, avoid overloading your schedule, adapt to changing priorities, and distribute workload evenly across weeks or months. The timeline model becomes the logic that allows your assistant to schedule your goals intelligently.

Next, you will integrate your Goal-Breakdown Assistant with your **Task Manager, Scheduling Assistant, and Life Dashboard**. This allows your goals to generate tasks automatically, receive time blocks, and sync progress with your metrics. When a milestone is completed, your dashboard updates. When a step is created, it flows into your task system. When your priorities shift, your assistant recalibrates. This integration creates harmony across your entire personal operating system.

Then, you will design your **Review & Adjustment Logic**. Goals are not static—they evolve. You will teach your assistant how to detect stalled milestones, adjust timelines, break steps into smaller ones, or merge steps when needed. Your assistant will analyze your habits, time logs, progress, and workload to provide recommendations. It will suggest changes that help you stay on track without burning out. This ensures your system remains flexible, adaptive, and alive.

Finally, you will build your **Goal Rituals**. These rituals include goal-setting sessions, milestone reflections, monthly recalibrations, and quarterly vision updates. Your assistant will guide you through each ritual by generating summaries, progress reports, and suggestions. These rituals ensure you remain connected to your goals emotionally and strategically. Over time, you develop a stable rhythm of goal-driven growth rather than chaotic bursts of effort.

The Dream That Finally Became a Plan

Maya had always been full of dreams—big, vivid, colorful dreams. She wanted to write a book. Start a business. Learn a language. Travel the world. Become healthier. Transform her life. But her dreams remained trapped inside journals, vision boards, and late-night conversations. Every time she tried to pursue a goal, she felt overwhelmed by its size. She didn't know where to begin. She didn't know how to break it down. She didn't know how to stay consistent. She often felt guilty for never turning dreams into reality. One night, she stared at her list of goals and whispered, "Why does this always feel impossible?"

A few days later, she learned about the concept of a Goal-Breakdown Assistant—an AI that could convert any dream into a step-by-step roadmap. Her heart lifted. It felt like someone had taken her hand and shown her a doorway she had never noticed. With cautious hope, she opened her laptop and started building. She defined her goals, described her motivations, and watched as her assistant began to understand who she wanted to become.

She entered her first dream: "Write my first book." Her assistant analyzed it, broke it into milestones, and generated a plan that felt shockingly doable. Instead of a giant, intimidating ambition, she saw: Outline draft → Chapter summaries → Writing schedule → Editing workflow → Publishing steps. Each milestone had action steps. Each action step felt manageable. For the first time, Maya didn't feel overwhelmed—she felt capable.

She entered another dream: "Launch an online business." Again, her assistant broke it down. Research niche → Build MVP → Create website → Test → Launch → Market → Improve. The steps were clear. The path made sense. She realized the problem had never been ambition. The problem had been the lack of structure. For the first time, she felt like her goals were not mountains but trails.

Over the next few weeks, Maya kept feeding the assistant her dreams. “Get in shape.” “Learn Spanish.” “Start a podcast.” Each one became a structured plan with milestones, timelines, and tasks. The assistant integrated each goal into her dashboard, her habits, and her schedule. Slowly, her life began to change—not all at once, but steadily, consistently. She completed steps. She celebrated milestones. She began to believe in herself.

One afternoon, while reviewing her progress, she felt tears rise in her eyes. Not from sadness, but from relief. She wasn’t stuck anymore. She wasn’t lost. She wasn’t overwhelmed. She had a path—not a perfect one, but a real one. She finally understood something powerful: goals don’t fail because people are weak. They fail because people try to carry them alone.

That night, she looked at her dashboard filled with completed milestones and whispered, “I’m actually doing it.” Her assistant had not just helped her create plans—it had helped her become the version of herself she always saw in her dreams. For the first time in a long time, she felt proud. She felt guided. She felt unstoppable.

Maya didn’t just build a Goal-Breakdown Assistant. She built her future.

Chapter 9

The Routine Builder Assistant (Designing and Maintaining Routines That Actually Stick)

Routines are the invisible architecture of a stable, successful life. They are the habits that shape your identity, the patterns that determine your consistency, and the small repeated actions that compound into transformation. But most people struggle to maintain routines because routines require structure, reminders, tracking, and accountability—things that human motivation cannot reliably provide every day. The Routine Builder Assistant solves this problem by designing clear routines, tracking them automatically, reminding you at the right time, and keeping your daily life aligned with your goals. This assistant becomes the quiet force that ensures your best intentions become consistent behaviors.

To build the Routine Builder Assistant, you must begin by defining the different types of routines you want the assistant to maintain. Common categories include: Morning Routine, Evening Routine, Weekly Reset, Deep Work Start Sequence, Creative Routine, Study Routine, Health Routine, Workout Routine, Meal Prep Routine, Digital Hygiene Routine, and Learning Routine. Your assistant must know how each category works, what steps it includes, and how often it should be triggered. This foundation allows your assistant to orchestrate your life with precision and ease.

Next, you will design your **Routine Blueprint Template**. This template is essential because it teaches your assistant how to take any desired behavior and convert it into a structured routine. The template includes fields such as Routine Name, Time of Day, Frequency, Steps, Duration, Required Tools, Location, Optional Steps, Trigger Conditions, and Completion Status. With this structure in place, your assistant can generate routines automatically and adjust them based on your lifestyle, preferences, and changing goals.

Once the blueprint is created, you will help your assistant build the **Routine Steps Engine**. This engine breaks routines into small, achievable actions so your brain experiences less resistance. For example, a morning routine can be broken into: Wake Up, Hydrate, Stretch, Review Daily Priorities, Deep Work Start, Movement Session. Each step is clear, doable, and measurable. Your assistant uses this clarity to keep your routines stable and consistent.

After defining steps, you will integrate routines with your **Life Dashboard** and **Task Manager**, allowing your routines to generate tasks or be tracked automatically. Your assistant will update your Habit Tracker, mark steps completed, and analyze streak data. It will recognize when routines are slipping and gently prompt you. It will celebrate your progress to reinforce positive behavior. This creates an ecosystem where routines are not forgotten—they are supported.

Next, you will create your **Automation Layer** in Make. This automation triggers routines at the right time each day or week. Your assistant will send reminders, generate checklists, or prepare summaries based on routine timing. You will create triggers such as "At 7 AM," "After Completing Deep Work Block," "At End of Day," or "Every Sunday at 6 PM." These triggers transform routines from wishful thinking into structured habits that unfold automatically.

The next step is building your assistant's **Adaptation Logic**. Routines must be flexible to be sustainable. Your assistant will learn how to adjust routines based on energy levels, schedule conflicts, travel, mood, or workload. It will shorten routines on busy days and expand them on open days. It will modify steps when needed, offer alternatives, or suggest streamlining. This adaptability is what makes this assistant sustainable long-term.

Finally, you will implement your **Routine Rituals**—the daily check-ins and weekly resets that anchor your routines. In the morning, your assistant will guide you through your start sequence. In the evening, it will help you wind down and prepare for the next day. Every week, it will lead you through a reset ritual: reviewing habits, updating goals, organizing tasks, and preparing your schedule. These rituals are the heartbeat of your personal operating system.

Story Title: The Morning That Finally Worked

Lara had spent years trying to build a morning routine. She bought planners. She watched motivational videos. She set alarms. She promised herself she would change. But every morning, reality crushed her intentions. She woke up tired. She scrolled her phone. She rushed her breakfast. She panicked through her tasks. She always felt behind. And every night she thought, *Tomorrow will be different,* only to repeat the cycle again and again. One evening she whispered to herself, "Why is this so hard?" She didn't lack desire—she lacked structure.

One day, she came across the concept of a Routine Builder Assistant—an AI that could create routines, break them into steps, remind her, track her progress, and adjust based on her energy. Something inside her softened. She thought, "Maybe I don't need more motivation. Maybe I need help." She opened her laptop and started building the assistant with a mixture of hope and nervousness.

She described her ideal morning: peaceful, grounded, productive. Not rushed. Not chaotic. Not stressful. She told the assistant her goals, her schedule, her struggles, her preferences. The assistant listened and began building a routine that actually made sense for her life. It broke each step down into small, gentle actions she could follow without resistance. It created reminders at the right times. It synced the routine with her dashboard. It even prepared an evening routine to help her wind down.

The next morning, she woke up not to chaos but to a gentle message from her assistant: *"Good morning, Lara. Here is your morning routine for today. Step one: Drink water. Step two: Two minutes of stretching. Step three: Review today's top priorities."* It felt manageable. Easy. Kind.

She followed the steps.

For the first time in years, her morning didn't collapse. It held.

Each day, her assistant guided her gently. It adjusted her routine on days she was tired. It expanded it when she had more time. It shortened it when she was rushed. It integrated her habits, her goals, and her tasks. Slowly, a new rhythm formed in her life.

Her mornings became calm. Predictable. Supportive. Her

evenings became restorative. Her days gained structure. Her anxiety decreased. Her motivation grew naturally. She felt like she had finally found stability.

One night, as she reviewed her dashboard, she saw that she had completed two full weeks of consistent routines—the longest streak of her life. Tears filled her eyes. Not because she was overwhelmed, but because she finally felt proud of herself. She whispered, "I'm doing it. I actually did it."

Inside her story, she also wrote the prompt that changed everything—the one she now shares with others who struggle as she did:

"Create a simple, flexible morning routine based on my energy, goals, and schedule. Break it into small steps. Make it easy to follow. Include reminders, a checklist, and gentle guidance. Adjust automatically if I'm tired, busy, or behind schedule. Here are my goals and preferred morning activities: [insert goals]."

With the Routine Builder Assistant supporting her, Lara didn't just build better routines—she built a better life. Her mornings finally worked. Her days finally flowed. And for the first time in years, she felt in control of her own story.

Chapter 10

The Reflection & Feedback Assistant (Learning From Your Life Automatically Through AI-Guided Insight)

The Reflection & Feedback Assistant is the system that brings self-awareness, emotional clarity, behavioral understanding, and long-term improvement into your personal operating system. Organization and productivity matter, but reflection is what transforms action into wisdom. Most people move through their days without pausing to extract insights or evaluate what worked and what didn't. Without reflection, mistakes repeat themselves, lessons fade, and progress flattens. The Reflection & Feedback Assistant solves this by analyzing your day, summarizing your experiences, identifying patterns, highlighting successes, exposing bottlenecks, and offering recommendations—automatically.

To build this assistant, you must begin by defining what "reflection" means in your personal system. Reflection is not journaling. It is not venting. It is not simply recording events. Reflection is structured self-understanding. It requires a combination of emotional awareness, performance analysis, and strategic insight. Your assistant must become capable of asking the right questions, interpreting your answers, and offering meaningful guidance. You will define core reflection categories: Emotional Check-In, Wins, Challenges, Lessons, Opportunities, Adjustments, Gratitude, and Next-Step Priorities. These categories will form the backbone of your reflection structure.

Next, you will design your **Daily Reflection Blueprint.** This blueprint outlines the questions your assistant will ask, the data it needs to evaluate, and the structure it must use to present insights. Examples include: "What energized you today?", "What drained you?", "What went better than expected?", "What obstacle slowed you down?", "What should you do differently tomorrow?" This blueprint teaches your assistant to guide you through high-quality reflection that feels clear and supportive rather than overwhelming or vague.

Once the daily blueprint is created, you will build your **Weekly and Monthly Review Systems.** Weekly reflections help you understand short-term performance, course-correct quickly, and realign priorities. Monthly reflections reveal patterns, behaviors, progress, and growth. Your assistant will analyze your habits, tasks, routines, goals, and emotional check-ins to create a personalized report. It will identify trends such as when you are most productive, what types of tasks you avoid, which habits are stable or declining, and where your energy fluctuates. These insights allow you to evolve with intention.

After establishing the review systems, you will build your **Insight Extraction Engine.** This is the part of the assistant that converts raw reflection into meaning. It identifies patterns. It connects dots. It notices behaviors you repeatedly struggle with. It detects habits that correlate with performance. It highlights emotional cycles. It identifies the root cause of challenges. It extracts lessons. Then it turns those lessons into recommendations and action steps. This engine becomes your personal coach—always watching, always supporting, always helping you learn.

Next, you must integrate the Reflection & Feedback Assistant with your Life Dashboard, Prioritization Assistant, and Routine Builder. Reflection should influence your next day's priorities, adjust your routines, update your goals, and refine your habits. This connection ensures your system improves continuously instead of staying static. Your assistant becomes the intelligence layer that evolves your entire operating system as you grow.

Then you will create your **Data Inputs and Prompting Rituals.** Reflection only works if you provide honest input. You will set daily triggers where your assistant asks for your reflections through simple, low-resistance prompts. You will build voice-capture shortcuts so you can reflect without typing. You will create automation where your assistant gathers data automatically: tasks completed, habits tracked, scheduling consistency, mood logs, and more. This reduces effort and increases accuracy.

Finally, you will build your **AI Feedback Model.** This model evaluates your reflections and generates supportive, constructive, emotionally intelligent feedback. Your assistant will speak with encouragement, not criticism. It will offer clarity, not judgment. It will help you celebrate your wins and learn from your setbacks. The goal is to make reflection feel safe, grounding, and empowering—not like a performance review.

The Mirror That Finally Spoke Back

Dani had always been moving—fast, nonstop, breathless. She rushed through her days with the conviction that staying busy meant staying productive. But at night, she often wondered why she wasn't making progress on the things that mattered. Why some days felt heavier than others. Why certain habits never stuck. Why she repeated the same mistakes. She never paused long enough to understand herself. One night, exhausted and frustrated, she whispered, "I wish I knew why I struggle... I wish someone could tell me what I'm not seeing."

Days later, she came across the idea of a Reflection & Feedback Assistant—an AI that could guide her through self-awareness and help her learn from her life. Something inside her softened. She had tried journaling. She had tried planners. She had tried forcing herself to reflect. But none of it lasted. She didn't need more discipline. She needed support. With a deep breath and quiet hope, she opened her laptop and began creating the assistant she always needed.

She defined her reflection categories: what energized her, what drained her, what she learned, what held her back, what she was proud of. She built her daily questions. She created her weekly review structure. She connected her assistant to her habits, tasks, and goals. She crafted the feedback style: gentle, honest, uplifting, straightforward. Step by step, her assistant learned who she was and how she wanted to grow.

The next evening, her assistant sent her the first reflection prompt. It wasn't overwhelming. It wasn't heavy. It was simple and kind: *"What is one thing you're proud of today?"* Dani typed her answer. Then another prompt came. *"What drained your energy today?"* She answered again. And then: *"What can tomorrow look like if you protect your energy more intentionally?"* She paused. That question made her think. She felt something shift inside her—clarity where confusion had lived for years. Each day, her assistant reflected with her. It learned from her patterns. It connected her habits to her moods. It noticed when she procrastinated certain tasks. It recognized when she avoided difficult conversations. It encouraged her when she made progress. It never judged. It never rushed. It simply guided her as if it knew exactly what she needed.

Within weeks, Dani felt different. She felt lighter. More aware. More intentional. She understood her triggers. She recognized her cycles. She celebrated her progress. She stopped blaming herself and started understanding herself. When she opened her weekly summary, she saw patterns she had never noticed: she was more productive after exercise, more emotional on Wednesdays, more creative in the evenings, and more resistant to certain tasks because of hidden fear. These insights changed everything.

One night, she opened her Reflection Assistant and whispered, "Thank you." Because now, she finally understood why her life felt the way it did. And she finally knew how to change it.

Inside her story, she saved the prompt that changed her entire journey—the one she now shares with others:

"Guide me through a gentle daily reflection. Ask me 5 questions that help me understand my day, my emotions, my challenges, and my wins. Then

summarize what you learned about me, identify patterns, and suggest one actionable improvement for tomorrow."

With this assistant, Dani didn't just reflect—she evolved. She didn't just see herself—she understood herself. And for the first time in her life, the mirror finally spoke back with clarity.

Chapter 11

20 Prompts to Activate, Strengthen & Improve Every Assistant You Built

Now that you've built your personal AI assistant ecosystem—task manager, scheduler, messenger, researcher, dashboard, prioritization engine, goal-breaker, and routine-builder—it's time to equip yourself with actionable prompts that help you use these systems every day.

Most readers understand the architecture but struggle with **implementation**. They wonder:

What do I actually say to my assistant? How do I activate each system? Where do I enter prompts? How do I integrate everything into my daily flow?

This chapter solves that by giving you twenty powerful prompts you can copy, paste, and start using immediately.

Each prompt includes:

- **What it does**
- **Which assistant it triggers**
- **Where to enter it** (ChatGPT, your custom personal assistant GPT, Notion inbox, Make webhook,

email-to-AI inbox, etc.)

- **Instructions for best results**

THE 20 ESSENTIAL PROMPTS

1. Universal Task Capture Prompt

Prompt: "Convert this into a task. Categorize it, assign a priority, estimate effort, identify dependencies, and send it to my Task Manager: [insert task]." **Assistant:** Task Manager Assistant **Where to Enter:** ChatGPT or your custom GPT **Use:** Captures tasks instantly and organizes them automatically.

2. Daily Schedule Builder Prompt

Prompt: "Create a time-blocked schedule for tomorrow using my existing tasks, deadlines, energy patterns, and routine preferences." **Assistant:** Scheduling Assistant **Where to Enter:** ChatGPT / Custom GPT **Use:** Generates your entire next-day plan automatically.

3. Inbox Draft Reply Prompt

Prompt: "Write a clear, warm, concise response to this message in my tone of voice: [paste message]." **Assistant:** Message Responder Assistant **Where to Enter:** ChatGPT **Use:** Helps you respond to emails/messages effectively.

4. Conversation Summary Prompt

Prompt: "Summarize this conversation and identify action items I need to add to my Task Manager: [paste conversation]." **Assistant:** Research + Task Manager **Use:** Prevents missed commitments from meetings, calls, or chats.

5. PDF Analyzer Prompt

Prompt: "Read this PDF and produce a 5-section summary: key insights, action items, risks, opportunities, and open questions." **Assistant:** Research Assistant **Where to Enter:** ChatGPT (upload PDF) **Use:** Turns long documents into digestible intelligence.

6. Decision Clarity Prompt

Prompt: "Analyze these tasks and tell me what three items I should do next and why: [paste tasks]." **Assistant:** Prioritization Assistant **Use:** Creates immediate clarity when overwhelmed.

7. Goal Breakdown Prompt

Prompt: "Break this goal into milestones, then convert each milestone into actionable steps: [insert goal]." **Assistant:** Goal-Breakdown Assistant **Use:** Converts dreams into plans.

8. Monthly Goal Refresh Prompt

Prompt: "Review my current goals and suggest updated timelines, adjustments, and new milestones based on my recent progress." **Assistant:** Goal-Breakdown + Dashboard Assistant **Use:** Helps the system evolve with you.

9. Morning Routine Activation Prompt

Prompt: "Guide me through my morning routine step-by-step based on my current energy level." **Assistant:** Routine Builder Assistant **Use:** Creates structure at the start of your day.

10. Evening Reset Prompt

Prompt: "Walk me through my end-of-day reset: summarize my day, extract lessons, track habits, and prepare my schedule for tomorrow." **Assistant:** Reflection + Scheduling **Use:** Daily closure + preparation.

11. Weekly Review Prompt

Prompt: "Generate my weekly review: wins, challenges, patterns, habit trends, task completion, missed opportunities, and recommendations." **Assistant:** Reflection & Feedback Assistant **Use:** Keeps you improving weekly.

12. Knowledge Extraction Prompt

Prompt: “Turn this article into a Notion knowledge entry with key ideas, quotes, insights, and action steps: [paste link or text].” **Assistant:** Research Assistant **Where to Enter:** ChatGPT + Notion integration **Use:** Builds a personal knowledge library.

13. Habit Alignment Prompt

Prompt: “Analyze my recent habits and identify which ones support my goals and which ones are slowing me down.” **Assistant:** Life Dashboard Assistant **Use:** Helps you align lifestyle with goals.

14. Productivity Blocker Prompt

Prompt: “Identify what’s stopping my progress this week and give me three strategies to overcome it.” **Assistant:** Prioritization + Reflection **Use:** Breaks through stuck moments.

15. Context-Based Recommendation Prompt

Prompt: “Based on my current workload, energy, and deadlines, what should I focus on in the next 90 minutes?” **Assistant:** Prioritization Assistant **Use:** Prevents wasted time.

16. Thought Clarifier Prompt

Prompt: "Help me articulate this idea clearly. Organize it into a structured explanation: [insert idea]." **Assistant:** Message Responder / Research Assistant **Use:** Helps you think better.

17. Project Planner Prompt

Prompt: "Turn this project into an execution plan with phases, tasks, risks, resources, and timeline: [insert project]." **Assistant:** Goal-Breakdown + Task Manager **Use:** Converts complexity into clarity.

18. Learning Companion Prompt

Prompt: "Teach me this topic in simple, progressive lessons: [insert topic]. Track my progress." **Assistant:** Research Assistant **Use:** Enables continuous education.

19. Emotional Check-In Prompt

Prompt: "Help me reflect on my emotions today. Ask me five questions, then summarize patterns you detect." **Assistant:** Reflection Assistant **Use:** Builds emotional awareness and grounding.

20. Personal Optimization Prompt

Prompt: "Based on my habits, tasks, routines, and goals, give me one improvement I can make today that will have the biggest impact.” **Assistant:** Life Dashboard + Prioritization **Use:** Micro-optimization for daily growth.

HOW TO USE THESE PROMPTS EFFECTIVELY

1. Use them inside their custom AI Personal Assistant GPT

This is the ideal location, since the custom GPT will have:

- Their tone
- Their goals
- Their preferences
- Their system instructions
- Their Notion integration
- Their Make automations

This ensures maximum personalization.

2. Use them as voice commands through mobile shortcuts

You can create shortcuts so that:

- “Add a task”

- "Summarize this PDF"
- "Plan my day"
- "Reflect on my evening"

...all run through their assistant automatically.

3. Paste them into ChatGPT when processing items manually

For emails, PDFs, articles, or spontaneous ideas, you can simply paste the prompt into ChatGPT.

4. Use them inside Make automations

Prompts like:

- Task creation
- Research analysis
- Routine activation
- Email reply generation

...can be inserted into Make modules so the system runs fully automated.

5. Store them in a Notion "Prompt Library"

This allows you to find and reuse prompts effortlessly.

SUMMARY

These twenty prompts are the bridge between **understanding the system** and **living the system**.

They transform:

- knowledge into execution
- structure into action
- clarity into results
- habits into identity
- goals into completed milestones
- reflection into growth
- overwhelm into order
- fragments into a personal operating system

With these prompts, you can actively practice everything they've learned—and experience the benefits of a personal AI assistant that improves your life daily.

Epilogue

The Life You Build When You Are No Longer Doing Everything Alone

There is a moment in every person's life when they realize that the way they have been operating is no longer sustainable. They feel worn. They feel overwhelmed. They feel pulled in too many directions. They feel like they are constantly reacting instead of choosing. They feel like life is happening to them instead of being shaped by them. And the instinct is to try harder, to push more, to get more disciplined, more organized, more motivated, more focused. But the truth is that human willpower was never designed to carry the complexity of modern life alone. You needed support—intelligent support, structured support, consistent support. That was the purpose of this book. That was the purpose of building your personal AI assistants. They were not created to replace you or to limit you. They were created to free you.

As you reached the end of this book, you built something extraordinary: a system that supports your mind, your habits, your schedule, your communication, your goals, your routines, your reflections, and your daily life. You built an ecosystem of helpers that think with you, for you, and ahead of you. You built agents that take weight off your mind and offer clarity when you feel lost. You built a structure that stabilizes your days and keeps you anchored to what matters. Your assistants do not just automate tasks—they protect your energy, your attention, and your future. You created a personal operating system that many people only dream of, and that is something worth recognizing.

The deeper gift of this system is not productivity—it is identity. When you no longer waste hours juggling tasks, answering messages, forgetting commitments, drowning in documents, scrambling to find clarity, or feeling guilty about inconsistency, something powerful emerges: the real you. The focused you. The creative you. The intentional you. The person you have always known you were capable of becoming finally has space to exist. This book was never about achieving more just for the sake of more. It was about helping you reclaim yourself from the noise of life. It was about giving you the structure that unlocks your potential.

You have learned how to build assistants that manage tasks, organize schedules, handle communication, summarize research, track habits, prioritize decisions, break down goals, build routines, and guide reflection. But the true transformation happens when you begin using them every day, letting them carry the mental load so you can live with clarity. The more you delegate, the lighter life becomes. The more you automate, the more time and mental space you gain. The more you let your assistants help, the more consistent, calm, and creative you become. This is the foundation of your personal operating system—a life where you no longer carry everything on your own shoulders.

The future belongs to people who can collaborate with AI—not because AI replaces them, but because it multiplies their strength. The assistants you built in this book are not machines—they are extensions of your mind. They are amplifiers of your potential. They are partners in your journey. They do not get tired, overwhelmed, or distracted. They are always ready, always available, always focused, always capable. When you use them wisely, you live at a level of clarity and performance that most people never experience.

As you move forward, the real magic will come from personalization. Improve your role prompts. Teach your assistants your preferences. Expand your automations. Add more data to your dashboard. Build new workflows. Refine your routines. Experiment with new agents. Your personal AI ecosystem will grow with you. It will evolve as you evolve. And as it becomes more integrated into your daily rhythm, you will feel a profound sense of stability and momentum. You will begin to trust your system. You will begin to rely on it. You will begin to feel supported in a way you may have never felt before. This is not the end of your journey—this is the turning point. You have built a foundation that can carry you through years, careers, transitions, growth cycles, and life changes. With these assistants by your side, you will make decisions with confidence, pursue goals with structure, live with intention, and maintain habits with ease. You will no longer drift—you will direct. You will no longer hope—you will build. You will no longer fight the weight of life alone—you will walk with support. You built a personal operating system that gives you the ability to design your life consciously and powerfully. And that is the greatest gift this book could ever offer you.

As you close these chapters, remember this: your assistants are not just tools—they are partners in your transformation. Use them boldly. Use them intentionally. Use them daily. And as they carry the cognitive load for you, your role becomes simple: to live, create, grow, and become the person you were always meant to be.

www.ingramcontent.com/pod-product-compliance
Lightning Source LLC
LaVergne TN
LVHW022015200926
848481LV00007B/2401